# INSIDE A

# POET'S HEART

# DEDICATION

This book is dedicated to the memory of
Keisha Facey
"Rest in peace."

And to the memory of my brother
Jason St. John Johnson
"I miss you, bro."
R.I.P

# CONTENTS

# ACKNOWLEDGMENTS

To my mother, Ezett Johnson, thank you does not begin to convey the gratitude I hold for you. Thank you for always being by my side and encouraging me, though it may seem annoying at times, I would have it no other way. You are my rock and my place of comfort, you're the reason I'm here. Your words give me strength and your undying love has made me the man I am today. Thank you!

To my friend, Kahlia Lawrence, you have been so unbelievable and supportive through this entire journey. Thank you. We have several adventures to go. Buckle up!

To my brother, Jesse Johnson, my confidant, the reason I know the things I know and do the things I do. Even though you're my brother you're like a father to me as well I thank God for you every day; I don't know what I would do without you. Thank you for always having my back, no matter what, and for being such a strong brother that I can always look to for advice and being confident that it will be sound words of encouragement.

To my son, Jabari Johnson, I know you're only seven months old right now, but you're everything to me and the reason I found renewed hope and inspiration. You motivate me to be the best father alive and work hard to give you the life I never had. Thank you!

To my Development Bank of Jamaica Limited family, words can't even express the love I have for you guys, for 15 years y'all have done nothing but nurture, protect, inspire and push me to be better, from my very first manager to the present one. I hope this book makes you guys very proud.

# INTRODUCTION

This is the introduction to a book of poems by Audley Johnson entitled Inside a Poet's Heart; the story below explains why I wrote this book.

**St. Matthew 25 vs. 14 - 18**

[14] For the kingdom of heaven is as a man travelling into a far country, who called his own servants, and delivered unto them his goods.

[15] And unto one he gave five talents, to another two, and to another one; to every man according to his several ability; and straightway took his journey.

[16] Then he that had received the five talents went and traded with the same, and made them other five talents.

[17] And likewise he that had received two, he also gained other two.

[18] But he that had received one went and digged in the earth, and hid his lord's money.

The talent for writing poetry I received from the lord, and I have made it my duty to use this talent and not bury it. Compiling this collection of poems has been by far one of the hardest things I have done, but doing anything considered your passion is worth it. Never waste your talents use them.

This Book consists of 68 pages; the writing form of the poems are rhyme, free verse and lyric.

For me (and I hope for you) the book is an adventure. I aim to please. Its furtive theme is the joy of imagining. Take a look inside the heart of a poet while enjoy being captivated by my thoughts and feelings.

# MY DAILY PRAYER

On my knees, I can always find you
No matter the situation I'm going through
The ups, the downs
You've always remained true
You are faithful despite what I do

My God you've always protected us from danger
Even when the enemy doesn't come in the form of a stranger
We've won again because you're a game changer
Failing us is just not in your nature

When I'm without; you provide
All my needs; you supplied
Feeling alone; you abide
Something's bad for me; you denied
Lord, please continue to be my guide

Thou art my hiding place
When destruction stares directly in my face
And I have to plea my case
So that the wicked people will be disgraced
But I will continue running this race
Because of your mercy and your grace.

# NEVER GIVE UP

Sometimes life gets hard
I have no idea what's next on the cards
But one thing's for sure I'll never drop my guard
Because of the past experiences that has left me scarred
And people that I eventually barred
So I have to stay focus whether foreign or my yard
I know one day I'll make it
Because I'm destined for the stars

Believe in yourself or your dreams will be marred
My doubts, failures need to be discarded
And at the same time, I'm sending my haters these regards
I'm on the road to success and Achievement Boulevard
So I got to stay alert and never let them catch me off guard
Because the shooters will pull up on you like Damian Lillard
So you'll never walk alone like Steven Gerrard
What you sow, will be your reward
That's the life I'm working towards
So I got to put my trust in the Lord
And make it known for the record

Dear God,
My deeds I'm asking you to measure
Whether it be work or leisure
And stay beside me forever
So I will never give up
Whatsoever the endeavor.

# THIS TOO SHALL PASS

A familiar place yet again
This feeling has become my friend
I can no longer pretend
That this could be the end
Haven't I been here before?
Not so long ago
Why life can't just let me be
My mind continues to mess with me

Do I have a choice not to go through this?
Something constantly seems amiss
Emptiness like a deep abyss
Hopefully, I will get the gist
To finally conquer this situation
Success is my only motivation
I will continue to fight to survive
Refused to throw away my life

How strong are these chains
That captivates me with all these pain
Like a slave, I'm going to run away
Then live to fight another day
What doesn't kill you?
Makes you stronger
Or makes you live longer
Just don't give up the fight
For your redemption draweth nigh.

# STILL I RISE

Bury me into the deepest of soil
Would never be able to dim my Joy
Like a plant that grows towards the light of the sun
My branches will always spring
When past sorrows look to find me
Let my soul make her boast in thee
As downtrodden as I am
Slaughter me not like a lamb
For these hands are made strong
And in the King's house, I do belong
For I am the son of Solomon


Days have come when I felt cast down,
But yet still I've never felt alone
Because your still voice walks beside me
And your ears are forever close to my plea
So I know I will always rise
With burning flames in my eyes
To dry up the tears from my cries


The hardest of situations fazes me not,
The path once took I've never forgot
The growing pains
The disappointments marred with stains
On the road to riches and fame
Still, I rise
And in future, I will settle the score
Or one day just before I go.

# LIFE IS SHORT

Sounds cliché, isn't it
Never saw this one coming I'll admit
You were just here for a little bit
Until life decided to split

Suddenly another one is gone,
That was recently born
Your family and friends left to mourn,
While feeling torn

The problem is we think there is time,
While we are alive in our prime
So we forget that in our downtime,
We should make memories that will last a lifetime

The father gave us three scores and ten.
That is all we get my friend
I surely hope you'll comprehend
That in the end
We only regret the time we didn't spend

I love you
Remember to tell them
From morning to pm
Choose not to condemn
Because life is worth more than a gem.

Dedicated to my Brother Jason St. John Johnson RIP

# FALLING INTO YOU

Where have you been?
You've entered into my life like a whirlwind.
With a touch as soft as a baby's skin
You've made me happy like kids on the weekend
How else can I explain this feeling within?
Where should I begin
I'd choose you
Even if you had a twin
I feel this time I'm going to win
You're all I need in this life of sin

I can't seem to go a day without you
And I know many will be wondering who
You've got me sticking close like glue
Now you've earned the title my boo
Just because the love had grown
Your true colours are shining through
And I'm enjoying the view
I'm glad I pursue
Hopefully, you feel the same way too.

# DARK SKIN GIRL

Come and listen to my thoughts
My honest feelings
In the eyes of many, you're appealing
When you're around, I feel like revealing.
The love, imprisoned in me
Should I let it out?
Would you notice me?

You walk by
Sometimes stopped by
Wonder if you notice me hiding a crush smile
Whenever you say hi
My face blush for awhile
Should I tell you?
Would you honestly listen?

Days go by still, I think of you,
Wonder if you feel the same way too.
You're the girl of my thoughts
The one I'd give my heart
I should tell you now
But you guessed it
The words won't come out.

# CRUSH ON YOU

Crush on you
Crush on me
It crushes me to see
I'm still not the one to be
Yesterday this crush started
It has not yet departed

This Crush is more than I can Handle
It burns me like a candle
The feeling blows me like a wind
The silence cuts up within
Should I speak of this unknown affair
Would you even care?

You have no notion of this crush
How much I want to touch
The thought of you makes me blush
Holding you would be so just
But I guess this is only a crush
And will forever be just such.

# HOW CAN I MAKE YOU HAPPY?

How Can I make you happy?
How can I show you I still care?
Do I have to move mountains?
Cry tears, streaming down my face.
Should I do things differently?
Try rekindling our love instantly?

How can I rock your world?
Make you forever my girl.
I still love you unconditionally,
Never hurt you intentionally.
Like the sun comes up in the morning
You smile so brightly
Like the sun goes down
Never like to see you frown

Yesterday you were by my side
Today I need you by my side
Tomorrow,
Never leave my side.

# MY BURNING HEART

This feeling that burns within
My light shining dimly
Where did this feeling come from
I was happy not too long…ago
Inside my heart
I can't help but fall apart
Why must things be this way?
Why must I even stay?

This heart of mine keeps burning
Made so many mistakes but keeps on learning
Emotional rollercoaster ride
My Passion refuse to die
How Can I contain so much pain?
Maybe there is so much to gain?
Sometimes I listen to this heart
Another time, I wish to discord
My Burning Heart
My deceitful heart
We're together from the start
Reminiscing until we part.

# A HEART IN EXILE

Being hurt is nothing new
Heart, I've forgotten how to use you
Things I've done made me refuse too
From cupid's bow, you've dodged every arrow that once
flew
My love has finally gone absent
And left me feeling screwed
Yesterday I painted my heart in shades of blue
From flowers of the loveliest hue
The colour of crimson won't do
Love has ruined me while hitting me with the flu
So many missed chances
I am to rue

My heart is a mere shadow now
Because of my lover's broken vow
I remember the last word spoken ciao
But I give thanks for grace anyhow
And will get pass this tempest somehow
Because God won't give me more than is allowed
For my harvest, I need to sow
No matter how misty the forecast looks just now
Along the shore, my sunset will wow.

# INSIDE A POET'S HEART

My words are free and cannot imprison
They flow through bars, as being written
You never know which side of me you're getting
These are my honest feelings I'm admitting
Love has never been kind to me
I keep forgetting

Nobody seems to see my pain
Only the opportunity for them to gain
These are the thoughts that keep drifting through my
brain
No sunshine
Rain
No strength
Drain
No success
Vain
No freedom
Chains
But in spite of it all
I stay in my lane
With a strong mentality to remain sane

I am the most real and will remain
Abel always and never Cain
Searching for that joy cannot be contained
The love cannot explain
After the failure I want to be ready to try again
Work hard and constantly attain
But play in between so I'll never strain
These are the things I hope to obtain
Or I'll forever live my life with much disdain.

# OLD FLAME

Here we go again
Where should I even begin?
Is there a future for us?
Are your intentions worth my trust?
Or maybe we're back here because of our lust.
Should I consider this opportunity as luck?
And forever in your love, I'll be stuck.
Just remember love takes time
And giving second chances are not a crime.
Outside it's a cold world
We all need someone arms in which to curl.

Building together this time around is a must,
So in the future, there'll be no rust.
We need work to adjust,
Or this whole thing will be a bust.
But greater is he that is within us,
So let's not worry or even fuss
Like an angry horse kicking up dust
But love each other and remain focused.

# ARE YOU STILL DOWN

Just here reminiscing on the days,
When we use to enjoy each other ways,
Now of late we don't even date.
Are you still down?
I don't want to stuck in the past,
Where others use to say we wouldn't last,
Would you give us another chance?
Are you still down?
Now tell me what I'm supposed to do,
If I can't get over you
Nothing else left to lose
Are you still down?
Now what could I do differently
To save you and me
Change my ways possibly
Are you still down?
Okay, let's get this straight,
How much more it's going to take
For me to tolerate the things you perpetrate
Are you still down?
And even when I tried harder,
I fall beneath further
My screams are loud
Are you still down?
Now upon til' today

You know I still love you anyway
With my feelings never play
Are you still down?
Now I'm at this crossroad again,
Still, see you as my friend
Tell me where I can begin
Are still down for me?

# MAKE SURE

When you walk away from your last love
Make sure leave behind what's above
Closed the door firmly and not a sort of
Walk away, don't look back unloved
Save me the pain from being tangled
Don't want to be caught up in a love triangle
Make sure
I can't seem to handle
Do what's necessary to dismantle
Some things, most things, everything
I'm giving you a perfect example
Make sure
Cut it down, shut it down from every angle
Hit the delete button and cancel
Do not leave even an inch of hope to dangle
That's just giving the past permission to strangle
To leave you empty with a heart that's trampled
Make sure
Close the deal
No matter how you may feel
Give yourself a chance to heal
Even when your ex is trying to appeal
Threatening you with things they might reveal
Be strong you're made of steel
I know the feeling is just too surreal
Make sure to end it and never kneel
Although the situation isn't ideal
Make sure
Sign and seal.

# LET HIM GO

Oh, darling, you think he's going to love you better?
Let him go
He loves you but his feelings don't show
Let him go
He's never there for you
Let him go
He gives you excuse after excuse
Let him go
He made you angry until you blow a fuse
Let him go
Compromise, he refuses
Let him go
He verbally abuses you to the ground
Let him go
He's never around
Let him go
He's taking you for a clown
Let him go
You're his queen without a crown
Let him go
You cry in the nights until early in the morning
Let him go
For him, your body is never calling
Let him go

The things he does are appalling
Let him go
He's never going to change for you my darling
Let him go
One day will come your prince charming
To have and to hold
Love him with all your heart and never let him go.

# TO WHOM IT MAY CONCERN

Dear Love bug,

I have no idea how to start this expression
But having you daily in my possession
Is the greatest gift I have without question?
Loving you is my only obsession.

When my skies were gloomy and grey
Your sunshine wipes the dark clouds away
That's the type of love I wish will stay
My humble prayer I would pray

Never met someone, so wonderful
Maybe I'm gullible
But I can't deny you're just incredible
Nat King Cole, unforgettable

I could go on forever about you,
And let who don't know wonder it's who
Because that's the least to me, it's true
As long as you remain my sweetest taboo.

Regards

# WE NEED TO TALK

This sentiment I will always fear,
These four words prompt much despair
I don't know how else I can make this clear
Do you believe in love with Cher?
The first verse of that song you will hear
It's been a long time coming, tears
I can feel the beat of my heart changing gears
I'm about to be lonely this time of the year

Just don't say what's on your mind
Maybe rethink and give it a little more time
I badly need you in these arms of mine
Ever thine, ever mine, ever ours
Arrives my final hour
Your love for me has lost all its power
What we had is dead, scatter these flower
I can't explain how things got this sour

Now I'm in this sombre mood
Because you are crude
I've never felt this screwed
My strength, joy needs to renewed
Hopefully in time the agony will be subdued
Or else my feelings shall start a feud
But in the end, this is what I conclude
You're someone I should've never pursued.

# LATE NIGHT SHENANIGINS

Lying next to you in the dark
When your skin softly encounters mine; it quickly leads to a
spark
Every position possible our love can never park
Your body has the answers to every question that I barked

My fingers now somehow come into play
While you assume the position; I continue to slay
Because I am the hunter and your body is the prey
Go hard or go home; that's what I heard her say
At this rate hopefully, we survive another day
Now I understand just why you're my bae
In my arms, you should forever stay

We don't need the light to express our feelings,
The lack thereof goes well with our sexual healing
Our passion has no limit, no ceiling
The love we share belongs to us, no stealing
That's why I have no problem revealing
This weapon that I have concealing
It makes things a bit more appealing
When finished know I am not leaving
Let's climax now
And enjoy what's left of the evening.

# UNBOTHERED

First things first
I'm for real
I could care less
About what you feel
I'm trying to be a better me
Go ahead and be a better you
Funny how I thought that
You were someone I knew
Now you're back
Acting all brand-new
I got places I need to be
And things I need to do
Than sitting around
And messing with you
You might think I'm bitter
But nah, we cool
I'm just cutting you off
Cold turkey
And be cruel
I'm just doing unto others
The golden rule.

# BLACK HISTORY

If I am no longer a slave
Why am I bound in chains?
No longer sweating in those fields,
To fuel my master's wheels
No more chains around my neck and feet
Just mentally within my reach
How far have my people come?
How far my ancestors ran
To get away from that sulking place
We are trapped  these days

My heroes didn't get lynched
For my future to be so dimmed
Brothers, executed
While the evidence to convict is being refuted
Martin Luther King had a dream
That one day all races will be a team
So why are the changes taking so long
Even after Obama came along
They'll tell you slavery has ended
But in Libya, human rights are being suspended
For a certain ethnic group
You don't care because it's not happening to you

So where are my civil rights?
Do you understand why we fight?
Who feels it, knows it.
That's why we decided to show it,
All lives matter they say
While black ones are fading away
All we want is repatriation
From all the insufferable situations
Peace and love for all my people
One love from all the evil.

# BLACK POWER

When you see me raise my fist in the air
It's to let you know I'm well aware
Where I stand in society
Walking alongside the high and mighty
You can't tell me I don't belong
Been fighting this struggle all along
If you don't like things I'm saying
Then maybe you shouldn't prolong
Don't love my skin colour?
Then hater be gone
Are you trying to bring this brother down?
Sorry, I'm strong
We have oppressed for many years
Our breakthrough won't be too long
Now you see why I got to fight?
Even if it means losing my life
You might think I'm looking for a stripe
Nah, things don't seem too right
Some people are going to discourage you
Others will understand my plight
Am not giving up, buckle up
Don't miss this flight
Malcolm X, Rosa Parks
And Martin Luther King
Marcus Garvey without confidence in life
You're twice defeated before you begin
So raise your fist in the air
We are black and proud
And we don't care.

# HAPPY MOTHER'S DAY

From conception until birth
Those nine months of pain shows your worth
Only a female can bring forth life upon this earth
With a mother's love and her tender girth
She will love you until the day you return to the dirt

She will nurture and watch you grow
And pray for you so that the blessings will flow
The way of life she will show
Because of her experiences, she will know
She loved you from hello
So to your queen everything you owe
Let her be your yesterday, today and tomorrow
It's the best way to go

In the eyes of a child, a mother is God
To those who don't understand it might seem odd
The right path she'll guide you to trod
If you don't follow then a correction from the rod
Parents, we should applaud
Because a mother should never be a fraud.

# POEM TO MY UNBORN CHILD

Writing a poem to my unborn child
Just in case I never get to see you
Reminiscing on your smile
And the many times you're going to cry
Bouncing baby child
Hope you'll be happy all the time

Thinking now of being
The best father I can be
Bad and good times
It will be just you and me
Day, month, year and the moment in time
Leaves me impatient all the time
Whether boy or girl
The Nine-month time I'll see

This Poem will never include
All I want to say to you
But I know you'll appreciate
These feelings I have for you
Because of whether morning, noon or night
I'll be there holding you tight
In my arms, giving you my charms.

# A GENTLE SOUL

An individual so charming
A smile so bright
Your presence so warming
Always saying HI
Never once saw you scowling
Your demeanour so adoring

Recently we learned of your battles
you fought them without being rattled
Never knew you were this strong
Fighting this monster all along
Even though you're no longer by our side
In our hearts, you'll always reside

Finally now my friend
We both know this isn't the end
Your earthly journey has passed
You did so with great honour and class
It's only goodbye for now then
Until we meet again.

Dedicated to Keisha Facey RIP

# MISSING YOU

Sometimes I wonder,
Do you ever think about me?
The times we use to be
Spending time you and me
Those walks along the sea
Peace and serenity

The time we thought,
Would never end
Do you remember back then?
The love was strong as it could be
Endless love poetry
Now it's a space
Meaningless escapades

Nights aren't the same
The Days are just as lame
Emotions running wild
As sad as a sick child
Will I ever rediscover me?
Is this our destiny?
Lost love can never found
Only broken wings that have flown.

# HE IS RISEN

He knew the day would come
Betrayed by a close one
The sounds of a rooster crow
Denied not by a foe
Peter went outside and wept bitterly
Because he had rejected Christ utterly
The one I kissed would be the saviour
Deceived by Judas behaviour
The soldiers took him to trial
He went without his disciples by his side

By this time the false witnesses had come
And the charges they found were none
But they took counsel to put him to death
Sentence to his last breath
And even when the Roman governor found no fault at all
Crucify him was the multitude call
And when Pilate saw he couldn't prevail
He washed his hands and walked away
See to it he says
And the crowd had their way

Hail the king of the Jews
They shouted, while his side they bruise
A crown of thorns was upon his head
And they crucified him
Jesus cried and gave up the ghost
Because he loved us the most
Then Joseph took his body and laid it in a tomb
He was dead many would assume
But the resurrection morning loomed
When they checked, he wasn't there
He is Risen and gone somewhere.

# WHAT IS LOVE?

Being there in the most difficult of times
Loving you no matter the signs
Just doing about anything
And expecting nothing in return
Even after giving you everything that I've earned
Love will forgive you after every hurt
Even after trampling my heart in the dirt
Love says to love one more time
Until your true love you've found
Many will search
And will never find
Love as unconditional as mine.

# POETRY IS NOT DEAD

From these thoughts, I have in my head

To the ink on the paper, coming from my pen

I write these lines for all words unsaid

From the sun rising in the morning

Until I lay down my head

No one sees the tears I shed

The daily hustle to earn my bread

So my offspring's will be fed

My poetry keeps me sane

From all of my unknown pain

I am free

No more chains

Is there a better way to express my heart?

When rhymes and melodies kick start

Poetry is not dead

I write and play my part.

# NO EXCUSES

Just be a grown-up about it

Own this!

You were wrong

And denied it for so long

You see, acceptance is the key

So you can heal

Most importantly to grow

Just let it go

It's time to start reflecting

No more deflecting

A changed person I'm projecting

Excuses are never no good

Even if misunderstood

Just be honest

Make yourself a promise

No excuses

With all confidence oozed.

# MORNING RAIN

Awaken by the sudden drops on my roof

I slowly reach over to pull you close

Your body chilled by the temperature low

Mine as warm as the fireplace below

The opposite seems to attract

Like the addition and subtraction in math

I started to caress around the waist on thee

While we listen to on bended knee

The rain dictated the pace

Like a storm, we begin to rage

It's wet both out and inside

And I know you understand why

Morning rain your drops are never in vain

I'll patiently wait for you to come again.

# MY TIME

Tick tick tick

My lifespan continues to diminished

I'm trying to make it

I forgot; to live, live, live

I know you can relate

To this, this, this

I'm giving everything

And still not rich

Oh, life!

Why must you be a bitch, bitch, bitch?

If only; I had one wish

Tsk, Tsk, Tsk

I've been told to wait my time

But I can't sit around and waste my prime

Being poor should be labelled a crime

Lord, please show me a sign, sign, sign

Or a new pathway

So I'll be fine, fine, fine.

# MY FOOLISH PRIDE

I don't know why I listened to you

Now I'm here looking like a fool

Lost a jewel

Because I thought It was cool

Not to apologize to you

Now my tears could fill a pool

Sometimes; love can be cruel

Use my experience as fuel

They don't teach this stuff in school

So don't lose the one you love

Because of pride

Your true feelings should never hide

Or you'll end up dying inside.

# DON'T DO IT

I know you feel like giving up
Throwing in the towel
But don't do it
There's a fight inside of you
So many have been there too
Problems are nothing new
Taking your life is not the answer
Don't end it all because of anger
And even in a depressed state
You can overcome it with a little faith
Get rid of the rope
No pills to the throat
Forget about writing a suicide note
"You can overcome this!"
And here I quote.


Dedicated to anyone battling depression

# SHATTERED

You left me in pieces
Not just my heart
But also my life
Missing are pieces from the puzzle
My confidence in a puddle
I am now a broken man
Your love I will never understand
Some would say that wasn't love
Anything but the above
It's time to restart; mending this heart
But where should I start?
When everything fell apart
Forgiveness and just let it go
Loving again won't be easy
Just so you know
Can you fix my heart?
And never depart.

# REMINISCING

It was scarcely visible in the evening twilight

When I decided to wander off down memory lane

Thoughts of you penetrated my brain

With the speed of a bullet train

Will fate have us together again?

That I may vanquish; my demons within

I miss holding you close

And smelling the sweet fragrance of your skin

The scent soothes my soul

Like flowers from spring

Our love was like the sunshine

But now it's all dim

I would give just about anything

To experience when it had all begin.

# I AM

I am like a river that runs deep

Silent I am

I am like a storm at sea

But you can rest in my eye

I am like a journey

Walk with me a thousand miles

I am as a lawyer

If you need me; I'll lie

I am like a child that misbehaved

If you beat me; I'll cry

I am like a prisoned bird

When you release me; I'll fly

I am a poet

Free me

I'll write.

# DON'T BE AFRAID OF MY LOVE

It's kind and gentle all the time

It's the truest, no lies

It's the finest of wine

It gets better with time

I'm here to love you

Here's why

Our love shall live and not die

I am your guy

No substitute, no standby

We're destined for great things

If you can submit; comply

My love, don't deny

Give me a try

Let me love you forever

With kisses, no goodbye.

# CRUEL INTENTIONS

I know you don't love me

Just pretending and soon will leave

I see your plans

You wear them on your sleeves

I hear what you're saying

Truth needs no belief

What the hell you think?

I am naive

Your intentions right now; make me peeve

Try to find someone else

You can deceive

Happy I saw this coming

I am so relieve

Just pack your shit now

Then you can leave.

# IT'S YOUR SEASON

Doesn't matter which of the four

It's your time

Receive it, soar

The blessings are starting to show

Your cup overflows

You're reaping now

Just what you sewed

At this point

It doesn't matter what goes wrong

You just overcome it with a song

It's your season

Give thanks despite the reason

You are blessed.

# SUCCESS THE BEST REVENGE

From rags to riches

You worked hard from the ditches

Long and narrow were the roads

Carrying the heavy loads

But here you are standing

Taking nothing for granted

For everything you've achieved

Just because you believed

Here is the blueprint for many to follow

Also the motto

Repeat after me

I shall rise from the shadow.

# CHRISTMAS WITHOUT YOU

It's the happiest time of the year

But not for me

Because I'll be without you

To me, this is nothing new

So I'll spend it with the crew

And family too

It will not be the same though

Like Christmas without snow

Or Santa without three ho's

Kissing underneath the Mistletoe

I'll be wishing upon a star

Like the three wise men coming from afar

For you to be home

My sweet honeycomb.

# CAST YOUR BURDENS ON HIM

These battles you are fighting alone

You can't win

Your troubles are so much

Where should you begin?

The pain you hide under your skin

So many setbacks there have been

Your problems are full to the brim

Why not cast your burdens on Him?

Every last one of your sins

Why?

Because He cares for you

To Him, this is nothing new

Let God hold you close

And He'll carry you.

# BROKEN

Somebody once told me

Broken crayons still color

But what about broken souls,

Do they still heal?

How about broken hearts,

Do they still feel?

You can achieve

Anything the mind can conceived

Start coloring again

Start healing again

Start feeling again

Being broken

Is a state of mind my friend.

# INSANITY

If loving you leads to insanity,

Let me never find my sanity again

Let me wander through life

Like a nomad

Lost for eternity

I don't need any therapy

I'm fine

With what your love has done to me.

# LADIES, KNOW YOUR WORTH

I know you're searching for love

But be patient

And love will find you

You long to be held close

By someone who loves you the most

You want to be wine and dine

Because ladies you are a dime

I know you see his lies

Let me get between your thighs

But you got to stop and visualize

You aren't taking me for a ride

Respect me

You're no longer going to sweat me

Self-love

Learn to put yourself first

Don't let him take advantage of you

Just because of your thirst

If this is a family trait

You can break the curse

I hope you understand

Every single one of my verse.

# I WILL LOVE YOU

I will love you until the end of time

Until we become immortals

Just so you know

If eternity should end

And starts all over again

Even then

I will

Love you all over again.

# AFTER THE HONEYMOON PHASE

After the thrill have subdued

And our love is no longer new

Will you still be my boo?

When everything starts falling through

Would you leave or stay like a statue?

At this point, I can see your true colors

Not all are wonderful like a flower

But I'm here to stay when it gets sour

Because I have tremendous will-power

And will love you until your final hour

So please tell me you feel the same

And you're not playing games

Your love has been tame

And not what others may claim

Then I shall give you my last name.

# PHOENIX MENTALITY

From the ashes, I'll rise

After being burnt to the ground

The former me, will not be found

And a new king will be crowned

Flames within

Have burn away the past

The future to be embraced at last

I see nothing but clear skies

As I spread my wings to paradise

Sometimes feeling the heat is a good thing

Your cup flowing over the brim

The choice is yours

Drown or swim?

Everybody has that hidden fight within

Or the courage to win built-in

Both are similar like a synonym.

# FOUR SEASONS OF LOVE

In spring my love begin growing from planted seeds
That blooms into flowers with scent leaves
It's a feeling that I'm glad to retrieve
Like animals with newborn to feed
Your presence brought a climate change
With emotions coming down like rain

In summer your love warms up my soul
Like the heat outside, that no one can control
Sun forge our love whole
Closing up all my hurts once in a hole
Summer love my heart you stole
The verdict is out; I need no poll

In autumn our love begin to fall
Like trees that go dormant everything stalled
Once a promising prospect hits the wall
Leaves falling and colors changing
Lovers become strangers such a weird thing
Wish we could go back to when it was spring

In winter our love froze
Like a homeless person outside without clothes
Who feels it, knows
You were just a heartless brat I suppose
Now I'm going to be just as cold
And my loving ways withhold.

Made in the USA
Middletown, DE
17 August 2022

71632522R00043